IRISH ELEGIES

IRISH
ELEGIES

MEMORABILIA OF

ROGER CASEMENT   THOMAS MACDONAGH

KUNO MEYER   JOHN BUTLER YEATS

ARTHUR GRIFFITH   MICHAEL COLLINS

THOMAS HUGHES KELLY   DUDLEY DIGGES

JAMES JOYCE   WILLIAM BUTLER YEATS

MONSIGNOR PADRAIG DE BRUN

SEUMAS O'SULLIVAN ALLEN, LARKIN & O'BRIEN

by

PADRAIC COLUM

INTRODUCTION BY LIAM MILLER

THE DOLMEN PRESS

Set in Baskerville type
and printed and published in the Republic of Ireland
at the Dolmen Press
North Richmond Industrial Estate
North Richmond Street   Dublin 1

Designed by Liam Miller

The first version of 'Irish Elegies'
containing six poems was printed in 1958
as the ninth part of 'The Dolmen Chapbook'

The second edition, with additional poems,
dated June 1961, was published in 1962

The third edition, reset, was published in November 1963

This fourth edition, with three additional poems and
an introduction, was first printed in September 1976

ISBN 0 85105 315 7

General distributors in the U.S.A. and in Canada :
Humanities Press Inc.
171 First Avenue, Atlantic Highlands, N.J. 07716

CONTENTS

INTRODUCTION

In 1956, not too long after I had established the Dolmen Press in Dublin, a letter reached me from Padraic Colum offering us his new poems. This generous gesture from an internationally acknowledged poet typifies Padraic's life-long dedication to serve, with friendship and devotion, the cause of Ireland, life and culture.

His ninety-year-long life spanned the emergence of the Irish nation. He was one of the earliest members of our National Theatre company and contributed to our theatre several of the most distinguished plays of its early years, among them his best-known play, *The Land*, which was first performed at the Abbey in 1905, the year that also saw the first production of Synge's *The Well of the Saints*. In the plays of his last years he returned to Irish themes, treated in a manner derived from the Noh theatre of Japan. Several of these last plays were broadcast by RTE and performed at Dublin's little theatres, the Pike and the Lantern. The first of these later plays, *Moytura*, was published at this Press in 1963 in a limited edition.

His career as a poet was firmly established by the publication in Dublin, in 1907, of *Wild Earth*, a volume which contains such well-known lyrics as 'An Old Woman of the Roads', 'A Drover' and 'A Poor Scholar of the 'Forties' which have been loved by generations of Irish people, as well as his best-known lyric, 'She Moved Through the Fair' which, as a folk song, has gone into the mainstream of our tradition and is sung by countless people who do not even know its writer's name.

Wild Earth was reprinted several times and was the first of many distinguished books of verse, the last of which, published by us in Dublin sixty-two years later, in

[7]

1969, was, perhaps prophetically, named *Images of Departure*. Novels, biographies and several well-loved children's books also came from his active pen.

Among the many awards and distinctions Padraic received for his poetry were, in 1940, the medal of the Poetry Society of America; in 1952, the Fellowship Award of the Academy of American Poets and, in 1953, the Gregory Medal of the Irish Academy of Letters, of which he was a founder member and, for several years, president.

In *Irish Elegies*, which he described as his 'memorabilia', Padraic sets down his tributes to men who illuminated his lifetime, a period which, as he said, was 'long enough to be historical'. The subjects of these poems reflect the range and quality of the poet's friendships — Roger Casement, Kuno Meyer, John Butler Yeats, Arthur Griffith, whose biography he wrote, and James Joyce all figure among those who formed part of his wide-ranging life. Speaking at Thoor Ballylee, which he opened as part of the Yeats centenary celebrations in 1965, he recalled many figures from his life. Many of us at the ceremony felt the extraordinary, almost epic quality of the then 84-year-old poet, who concluded the ceremony by reading his own elegy for W. B. Yeats which is now included in this volume.

In 1970, when Padraic left at the end of his annual visit to Dublin, he promised to come again in the winter. He was working on his autobiography. Illness came to him during a lecturing engagement and he was to spend his remaining time with his body stricken. But his active mind carried on to the very end, planning new poems and dictating his memoirs. Padraic Colum died at Enfield, Connecticut, on 11 January 1972 and was buried in Ireland on 18 January.

LIAM MILLER

[8]

IRISH ELEGIES

WRITTEN *over a period long enough to be historical, these pieces are tributes to men who illuminated the period. They are less elegies than memorabilia : each, produced immediately on the announcement of death, came out of a realization that the one whose passing was noted had augmented the Irish spirit in formative years. Each man contributed to a movement and took character from it. They were all touched by the passion that is in Irish history and was perhaps more present in their day than since or before.*

This does not apply to a particular elegy. A generation grew up with the recollection of the three who died with 'God Save Ireland' on their lips, and it was in piety to the fathers and mothers of that generation that the memorabilia of Allen, Larkin and O'Brien was set down.

DUBLIN 1958-1967

[9]

THE REBEL

ROGER CASEMENT

1864-1916

They have hanged Roger Casement to the tolling of a bell,
Ochone, och, ochone, ochone!
And their Smiths and their Murrays and their Cecils say
     it's well,
Ochone, och, ochone, ochone!
But there are outcast peoples to lift that spirit high,
Flayed men and breastless women who laboured fearfully,
And they will lift him, lift him for the eyes of God to see,
And it's well, after all, Roger Casement!

They've ta'en the strangled body and laid it in the pit,
Ochone, och, ochone, ochone!
And brought the stealthy fire to waste it bit by bit,
Ochone, och, ochone, ochone!
To waste that noble stature, that grave and brightening
     face
That set courtesy and kindliness in eminence of place,
But they — they'll die to dust that no poet e'er will trace,
While 'twas yours to die to fire, Roger Casement.

THE POET-CAPTAIN

THOMAS MACDONAGH
1878-1916

How shall I show him? How his story plan?

This you asked for him, the man in your first play,
And for another audience I ask this:
How shall I show you, how your story plan?

    An excursion train
That's journey-bound for pilgrimage
Or tournament — I'll place you there.
The landscape changes, humours change,
And you who talked to thoughtful men
Of Villon, or of Horace, or
Of wild Catullus and his love,
Now raise for us a parish song
That brings to life the folk of those
Odd houses at the boro's end —
Local as jackdaws on the roofs
Of some small Tipperary town,
Lively as jackdaws on the slates,
And you, remarked for pompousness
Will be acclaimed for drollery.

How shall I show you? How your story plan?

In Saint Canice's: we walk down
An aisle and find ourselves beside
An effigy in black limestone
Of knight recumbent — here you speak
Of figure you have mind to form.
All we who carry banners dream,
And try to put our dream in text
Of play, or poem, or history.

[12]

This dream of yours you'd bring to life
Upon a stage. The hero? Who?
Someone in time that's yet to come —
The Poet-Captain who'll transmute
The word into the deed, the deed
Into the vibrating word.
The play I saw remembering
The chapel-aisle, the lonely knight
Whose word was in a language gone
As word on shield. I ask again —

How shall I show you? How your story plan?

You step into our company
In kilts and *brat* and with a brooch
As good as plume for gallant show,
And tell us poems will add to poems
Are in your scrip, and tell them well.
The Yellow Bittern, never out
In drinking bout is dead beside
The bog-drain that was all his booze:
He might have had a flightier life.

John-John is back to card-trick men
And maggie-men at Nenagh Fair —
Not for the like of him a house
And household chores. Unseen, unheard
The dogs hunt over untracked field
At night, and have unkennelled life
Their sleepy owners cannot know.
Then from those earlier, I recall
An April verse —

The songs that I sing
Should have told you an Easter story
Of a long sweet Spring
With its gold and its feasts and its glory.

How shall I show you? How your story plan?

Court-martial. Now you come before
The men with power of dealing death:
You speak to them of trialled man,
Of Savonarola, Florentine.
(And who but you would bring that name
Before a bench of medalled men?)
They judge you by their printed book.
Then in the barrack-yard you prove
That your own judgement's unrevoked —
The Poet-Captain; there you tear
From history the double word,
The envoi to your poems!

THE SCHOLAR
KUNO MEYER
1858-1919

Arch-scholar they'll call you,
Kuno Meyer —
The men of learning . . .
But who will tell them
Of the blackbird
That your heart held?

On an old thorn-tree
By an ancient rath
You heard him sing,
And with runes you charmed him
Till he stayed with you,
Giving clear song.

He sang o'er all
That Maravaun
Told King Guire;
And he told you how
Bran heard the singing
Of a lovely woman
And sailed for Faerie;
And of how slain princes
Kept tryst with women
Loved beyond
The pain of death,
In days when still
The boat of Mananaun
Bore towards Eirinn!

Arch-scholar they'll call you,
Nay, Rune-Master!
You read in texts
Not words only
But runes of old time;
And when you spoke them
A curlew cried
Over grass-waste Tara,
And a cuckoo called
From the height of Cashel,
And an eagle flew
From Emain Macha!

Ochone, ochone
That we'll see no more
In the Eastern or
The Western World
Your great head over
The lectern bending
Nor hear your lore
By a pleasant fireside.

But the runes you read
Have given us more
Than the sword might win us:
May kind saints of Eirinn,
Kuno Meyer,
Be beside you
Where birds on the Living
Tree sing the Hours!

THE PAINTER
JOHN BUTLER YEATS
1839-1922

'To-night,' you said, 'to-night all Ireland round
The curlews call.' The dinner-talk went on
And I knew what you heard and what you saw,
That left you for a little while withdrawn —
The lonely land, the lonely-crying birds!

Your words, your breath are gone!
O uncaught spirit, we'll remember you
By those remote and ever-flying birds
Adown the Shannon's reach, or crying through
The mist between Clew Bay and Dublin Bay!

Your words, your breath are gone,
I, careless, said. But your live eyes, live hand
Have left the pictures of these noted men,
So many, and so filled with wakefulness
That voices from them pass above the land.

THE STATESMAN

ARTHUR GRIFFITH
1872-1922

You had the prose of logic and of scorn,
And words to sledge an iron argument.
And when the words were in their metals braced,
There were the street and country songs for you.
You were the one who knew
What sacred resistances in men
Are almost broken; how, from resistance used
A strength is born, a stormy, bright-eyed strength
Like Homer's Iris, messenger of the gods,
Coming before the ships the enemy
Has flung the fire upon. Our own, our native strength,
In days of garrulous men you mustered up.

And sorrow comes as on that August day
With our ship cleaving through the sea for home,
And that news coming sparkling through the air,
That you were dead, and that we'd never see you
Listing the tasks would make a country nobler,
Honoured by men who knew the love you bore them.

And could we pray, reaching the island homeland,
Other than this, 'Odysseus, you who laboured
So long upon the barren outer sea —
Odysseus, Odysseus, you who made
The plan that drove the wasters from the house,
And bent the bow that none could bend but you:
Be with us still:
Your memory be the watcher in our house,
Your memory be the flame upon our hills!'

THE CHIEFTAIN

MICHAEL COLLINS
1890-1922

A woman said, 'He would sit there,
Listening to songs, my mother's sheaf,
And he would charm her to regain
Songs out of note for fifty years,
(Did he remember the old songs?)
For he was of the mould of men
Who had renown in her young days,
The champions of cross-roads and fields.'

> (His head as like the head upon
> A coin when coins were minted well,
> An athlete passing from the games
> To take his place in citadel.)

'But once I saw a sadness come
Upon his face, and that was strange —
The song she sang had less of fret
Than all the rest — a Milking Song,
(Did he remember the old songs?)
A girl's lilt as she drew streams
Into her pail at evening fall.
But you would think some great defeat
Was in his mind as she sang on.'

> (Some man whom Plutarch tells about
> Heard in the cadence of a song
> The breaking of a thread, and knew
> The hold he had was not for long.)

'Only that once. All other times
He was at ease. The open door
Might show no danger lay across
That young man's path as he sat there,
Listening to songs of the old time
When songs were secret in their hope.
(Did he remember the old songs?)'

    (A strategist, he left behind
    Pursuit each day and thwarted death
    To plan campaign would leave no name
    To field nor to a shrine a wreath.)

But she had seen upon his face
Something that danger could not cause
Nor could she guess: the fateful glimpse
On instant opened to the man
Summoned by history. He will know
While someone outside lilts the words
That have no fret, that he must choose
Between what forceful men will name
Desertion, but that he'll conceive
As action to bring fruitful peace
And see (it could be) rifle raised
Against deserter who had led.

    (Who breaks into a history breaks
    Into an ambush frenzy-set,
    Where comrades turn to foes, and they
    The clasp of comradeship forget.)

'Did he remember the old songs?'
She asks where requiem leads us on
By quays, through streets, to burial-ground.
I answer from my searching mind,
'His powers made him prodigy,
But old devotions kept him close
To what was ours; he'd not forget
Threshold and hearthstone and old songs.
The requiem made for divers men
Is history; his music was
The thing that happened, as said Finn.'
'No one is left on Ireland's ground
To hear that music,' she intoned,
'Since Michael Collins walks no more.'

    (The citadel he entered in
    Without procession or acclaim
    And brought a history to an end,
    Setting his name 'gainst Norman name.)

THE PILGRIM

THOMAS HUGHES KELLY

d. 1933

I dreamt my friend had come into a room,
Where I had chided him for tasks delayed,
And he had said in answer to that blame:

'I was a Pilgrim and to many lands —
Not shrines too many, for in each there was
Some grace to be recalled to other men,

And I was chosen to recall that grace,
Although it meant 'twas often mine to watch
My hopes disperse like beach-alighting gulls.

I was a Pilgrim, and though all I planned
As I went far and near has left scant trace,
The blessings that I gained are not out cast —

They have annealed.' So I was answered well:
The purpose that was natal marked his face,
And he was raised as with a prime of strength

That matched the bounty that was his; I knew
He had been chosen for a task beyond
Our world's ken, and had accomplished it.

THE PLAYER
DUDLEY DIGGES

d. 1933

who played opposite Maud Gonne
in the first production of Kathleen ni Houlihan

The candles lighted and the figure prone
Announce this to you: they are laid aside,
The noble, whimsical and pathetic roles
Disanimated, not to be resumed!

A hush that's not expectancy is here.

Old dreams, old songs, old prophecies became
A fateful gesture, when he turned around
Knowing the houseless woman for the Queen,
And Father, Mother, Bride held him no more.

The solemn knocks are not for curtain's rise.

The lifelong role
Of instant goodness and deep faithfulness
Beyond the curtain fall will be sustained
And the heart's theatre keep lease of play.

THE ARTIFICER

JAMES JOYCE
1882-1941

The long flight and asylum barely reached —
Asylum, but no refuge from afflictions
That bore on you and left you broken there —
This was the word was brought me: loneliness
That was small measure of the loneliness
That, days and nights, was with you, came to me.

Daedalus! Has your flight ended so?

I looked back to the days of our young manhood,
And saw you with the commons of the town
Crossing the bridge, and you
In odds of wearables, wittily worn,
A yachtsman's cap to veer you to the seagulls,
Our commons also, but your traffic
Sombre: to sell your books upon the quay.

And then, with shillings flushed,
To Barney Kiernan's for the frothy pints,
And talk that went with porter-drinkers there.
But you
Are also Schoolman, and these casual men
Are seen, are viewed by you in circumstance
Of history; their looks, their words
By you affirmed, will be looked back on,
Will be rehearsed. Nor they, nor I
Nor any other, will discern in you
The enterprise that you in secrecy
Had framed — to soar, to be the man with wings.

We did not know
The searching eyes beneath the peak of cap
Beheld
The Seventh City of Christendom
Re-famed. We did not know
Below your sayings there was incantation
To give the river back to twilight field,
River of discourse,
                  Anna Livia,
River of fable,
              Plurabelle.

THE ARCH-POET
WILLIAM BUTLER YEATS
1865-1939

Since he who kept us proud for two score years
With verse and speech is into silence gone,
No eloquence!
            But candles will avail:
They are more fitting to our hushedness!
           And first
The candle that was sconced in curtained room
By one so shy, her motions were a plea
To be restored to that lake-island where
The wren and robin kept their heritage
Of quiet. And bring us, too,
The candles were above the altar rails
Where country girls knelt, while, through their prayers
The songs a sinful man made for a girl
The like of one of them, came
Like the warm drippings from below the wicks.
           But he
Had crossed our frontiers, and had read the books
Of Paracelsus, and his gains were known:
Initiate's knowledge, fabulous discipline
In starlit poems. So we will bring
The gentile tapers from the Mountain Tomb
Where Father Rosicross,
The Magus's and Sophist's wisdom closed
Within his eyes, and music and wine,
Dancing, and lips kissed waste day and night,
While cataract sounds upon the mountain side.

But voices only here : we'll speak of him
As persons speak to persons in a room :
A man of vision and a man of wit,
And constancy, and one who kept beneath
All that was noted in him, all
Of phrase and mask, discourse, accomplishment,
Steadfast affections, and was happily
In places shared with sisters and with brother —
Collooney, Ballysodare,
Drumcliffe and Moherbui and Dromahair.

THE MAGISTER

MONSIGNOR PADRAIG DE BRUN
1889-1960

Since Yeats his eagle mind
Resigned, our household grows
Less and less genial:
They leave who kept us proud.

No more can we retail
The wit lyric vein —
Seumas O'Sullivan's,
Nor meet the spray that dashed
From seas are Mananaun's
Through Stephens' resource.
Nor catch the quips, the japes,
The poetry in flights
That were Gogartian,
Nor in the affable
Scholarship was Best's
Can we have any part:
Our household poorer grows.

And now is gone from us
That master of discourse
Who moved in realms of art,
Science, philosophy;
Who could outrange the bards
With verse he had in mind,
And yet could keep the pitch
Of humours of the street:
They leave us one by one!

[28]

Even he whose presence showed
The plenitude within —
The eagle in his look,
The manfulness of height,
The voice like Corrib flow
When poetry was theme —
The Gaelic dark and deep,
The Latin swift and strong,
Star-lit Italian,
And English in cascade.
But, no! We cannot lose,
Although we know who's gone,
That man of ours who had
All wit could animate,
All memory could provide!

THE POET
SEUMAS O'SULLIVAN
1879-1958

Montaigne — the last words that I heard you speak
Were that old man's, and I was made elate
To know that one I left upon the street
Was still attuned to that astringent mode.

Fastidious, elegant. And then my mind
Went back to times when youth was doubly youth
With graft of blossoming poetry upon it.

And you would speak your poem as though abashed
To bring a child so gentle through a crowd.
But though averted, lightened were your eyes —

And that no wonder, for they kept the quest
To 'learn the things old times have left unsaid',
Gathered, maybe, beside where sedges bowed,
Or near a tarn where a lone heron cried.

THE FENIANS

'Pray for the souls of Allen, Larkin and O'Brien.'
Such names as might be found on any street
I read in prayerbook leaves of long ago.

Pray for their souls! I hear petitions rise
By hearths, in chapels, and by open graves
Where men the names repeat beside their brothers'.

The three doomed men! They turned and made appeal
To cause beyond the disdain of their judge,
Then left their bodies to an unmarked grave,

And their names to an utterance: their scroll
Will not be torn nor their tablets razed
Whose memory in fervent words abides.

Pray for their souls, and for theirs, one and all
Who gave a thought, a deed to Ireland's gain.

AVE ATQUE VALE

Thorough waters, thorough nations I have come
To lay last offerings at your low abode,
Brother, and to appeal
To ashes that were you.

Since that which none can check has borne you
From my regard, poor brother, take these gifts —
The tokens that are due
To ancient pieties.

But they are wet and over-wet with tears,
With brother's tears : and now I say farewell —
Henceforth and for all time,
Hail, brother, and Farewell.